1 MONTH OF
FREE
READING

at

www.ForgottenBooks.com

By purchasing this book you are eligible for one month membership to ForgottenBooks.com, giving you unlimited access to our entire collection of over 1,000,000 titles via our web site and mobile apps.

To claim your free month visit:

www.forgottenbooks.com/free1013634

ISBN 978-0-331-09476-3
PIBN 11013634

ASSESSMENT SYSTEM.

ONS OF SCOTLAND

Benevolent Society.

CONSTITUTION

—OF THE—

rand Camp & Subordinate Camps

(INCORPORATED)

GRAND CAMP

ORG. JUNE 27
1876.

TORONTO,
ONT.

SONS OF SCOTLAND.

Lealty, Loyalty, Liberality.

BELLEVILLE.

INTED AT THE ONTARIO BOOK AND JOB PRINTING HOUSE,

ASSESSMENT SYSTEM.

SONS OF SCOTLAND

Benevolent Society.

CONSTITUTION

—OF THE—

Grand Camp & Subordinate Camps

(INCORPORATED)

GRAND CAMP

ORG. JUNE 27
1876.

TORONTO,
ONT.

SONS OF SCOTLAND.

Lealty, Loyalty, Liberality.

BELLEVILLE.

PRINTED AT THE ONTARIO BOOK AND JOB PRINTING HOUSE

OUR AIMS AND OBJECTS.

Our Native Land-Our Adopted Country-Our Brotherhood.

ADDRESS TO SCOTCHMEN.

Every man has a peculiar love for the land of his birth and
the home of his ancestors. He may have been born in a land
unhonored by fame and unsung in story, nevertheless he delights in it as the land of his nativity. His home may have been
the burning sands or the snow-clad plains, the fertile valley
or the barren mountain, the fragrant vale or the desolate
waste, the thinly populated country or the densely crowded
city (it matters not how varied the scene) yet it has a charm
for him which no foreign land can alienate and no clime de-
stroy. This patriotic virtue is one of the noblest character-
istics of the human race. It has been extolled and applaud-
ed in every age, and he who becomes a traitor to this sacred
tie is scorned and despised by all. Such were the sentiments
of our own Sir Walter Scott when he says : —

" Breathes there a man with soul so dead." etc.

Though what has been said may be true of all nationalities
nevertheless the Scotch, in a greater degree perhaps, than
any other race, are wrapped up in the love and patriotism of
their native land. This state of feeling may be accounted
for in different ways. Scotland has for many centuries pro-
duced men who have taken the lead in every sphere of life—
men who have led the van in the reformation of religion and
politics, and whose names will never die. The names of her
warriors, poets and philosophers will live while the world
endures. For her renown in literature, and architecture
Edinburgh has been styled " Modern Athens." Nature has
not only lavished upon Scotland the beauties of mountain and

glen, but it has also given her a genial climate and a long summer day, which has tended greatly to the encouragement of outdoor sports, games and amusements. Combine the whole, and can it be wondered that the patriotism of a child of such a land should rise, not only higher than that of the serf of the tyrant, or the rude barbarian, but even above the patriotism of the citizens of civilized nations who have not shown any great desire to ameliorate the sufferings of their countrymen or actively to participate in any great movement for civil or religious reform? Thus circumstanced, the Caledonian leaves his native land with his mind full of sacred and historic memories, and his heart full of regret and emotion. His feelings then cannot be better expressed than by reference to those beautiful and pathetic lines by Thos. Pringle, when he says:—

"Our native land—Our native vale—
   A long and last adieu !
Farewell to bonny Teviotdale
   And Cheviot's mountains blue,
The battle mound—the Border tower,—
   That Scotia's annals tell—
The Martyr's grave—the lover's bower,—
   To each—to all—farewell !"

A Scotchman, when he arrives in a foreign land, finds little to cheer or to comfort, and his mind, therefore, delights to look back on the associations of his native land. His early training has enamoured him with the beauties of her literature ; his youth has been charmed with the grandeur of her scenery ; the recollection of many a noble intellect floats in his memory ; the sports, games and amusements of his childhood are still dear to him ; and though he cannot replace the friends and associations of his native country, yet he finds in his own countrymen elements capable of alleviating his sorrow and contributing towards his loss even in a foreign land. Their language, habits, customs and manners, are either the same, or very similar to his own, and in associating with them he feels more at ease and at home than he could possibly do with foreigners, whose ways of living, thinking and affections are totally different ; and he, therefore, very naturally seeks to form organizations in which these associations and memories may be kept alive. But hitherto every Scottish Society has failed to meet the wants of Scotchmen and their descendants in Canada. To meet their wants, this society, the Sons of Scotland, has been formed : but though formed specially for Scotchmen and their descendants in Canada, nevertheless it will readily accommodate itself to other foreign countries. Its objects are to cultivate a taste for Scottish music, poetry, history and general literature ; to encourage the wearing of the national costume and the practice of athletic games, sports and amusements ; to promote and maintain a love and kindly feeling for one another, and to provide a scheme to administer to the wants of the sick and the destitute, the widow and the orphan, and the burial of the dead. This assistance will not be given as a charity, but as a right, founded on the principles of a mutual benefit association It is believed that the pursuit of these objects will result in the development of the intellect, the perpetuation of the Scottish national costome and games, in bringing Scotchmen and their descendants more closely together, and in working a scheme that will, to a very great extent, render each member independent of charity.

The Grand Camp has endeavoured to frame the Constitution in such a manner as to form a great fraternal unity in the order, without interfering unduly with the rights of members of Subordinate Camps. The Constitution contains only such general principles as are applicable to the whole Order ; it will, therefore be the duty of each Subordinat Cnmp to pass such by-laws as its own circumstances may require for the carrying out of all the objects of the Association.

By a strict adherence to the Constitution and By-laws the Grand Camp is fully persuaded that the objects of the Order will be fully relized and that at every gathering or meeting the members will ever be found carrying out the moral sentiments of that beautiful melody of Robert Burns when he sang :—

> " Should auld acquaintance be forgot,
> And never brought to mind ;
> Should auld acquaintance be forgot,
> And days o'lang syne ? "

PREFACE.

THE GRAND CAMP OF THE SONS OF SCOTLAND, under and by virtue of a resolution passed in Robert Burns Camp, No. 1, of the Sons of Scotland, on the fifteenth day of August, one thousand eight hundred and seventy-eight, and then and there supported by the members of Robert de Bruce Camp, No. 2, and St. Andrew's Camp No. 3, which said Resolution was in the following words, that is to say :

Whereas, The Robert Burns Camp of the Sons of Scotland, has by resolution, duly moved and carried, given its consent to the opening of two other Camps, the one to be located in the western part of the city of Toronto, and to be known as the Robert de Bruce Camp of the Sons of Scotland, and the other to be located in the eastern part of the city of Toronto, and to be known as St. Andrew's Camp of the Sons of Scotland, and

Whereas, in order to form a perfect fraternal union, to establish order, to ensure tranquility, to provide for uniformity of initiation and conferring degrees, to promote the general welfare of the Order, and secure to the Sons of Scotland all the benefits, advantages, and blessings, of camp privileges, it is necessary that a Grand Camp should be formed and established having jurisdiction over all the Subordinate Camps wherever the same may be organized.

" *Therefore be it resolved*, That the Grand Camp of the Sons of Scotland be composed of the past Chiefs and present elective officers of the several Camps above mentioned, and that the Grand Camp be instructed with full powers to draw up a Constitution for the guidance of the Grand and Private Camps."

THEREFORE, the Grand Camp of the Sons of Scotland enacts as follows. (Then followed a copy of the original Constitution.)

By resolutions of the Grand Camp meeting, at Hamilton, in August, 1885, and Collingwood in 1887, several amendments and additions were made to the Constitution, as originally adopted in 1878.

At the Grand Camp meeting held at Barrie, in 1890, Brothers D. F. McWatt, John Galbraith, and F. M. Montgomery, were appointed a committee on Laws and Ritual. The results of their labors were submitted to the Subordinate Camps in 1890, and discussed at the Grand Camp meeting held in Robert de Bruce Camp room, Occidental Hall, Toronto, on February 3rd and 4th, 1891. The Constitution as then adopted by the Grand Camp, and put into form by the Laws and Ritual Committee, Grand Chief and Grand Secretary, is now presented to the brethern and comes into immediate operation, superceding all other constitutions and By-Laws of the Order hitherto in force.

    D. McCRAE,   WM. BANKS,
           GRAND CHIEF.   GRAND SECRETARY.

June 1st, 1892.

CONSTITUTION OF THE GRAND CAMP

OF

THE SONS OF SCOTLAND

BENEVOLENT SOCIETY.

NAME AND POWERS.

SECTION 1.   The Sons of Scotland Benevolent Society shall consist of the Grand Camp and Subordinate Camps.

SEC. 2.   The Grand Camp of the Order is the fountain from which springs all true and legitimate authority over Subordirdinate Camps.

SEC. 3.   It shall regulate and control all forms, ceremonies, written and unwritten work, change, alter, or annul, and provide for the safe-keeping and uniform teaching and dissemination of the same.

SEC. 4.   It shall provide and furnish all lecture-books, dispensations, charters, emblems, certificates, clearances, seals, regalia, etc., or order the same.

SEC. 5.   It shall issue the pass words, regulate the mode of using the same, and establish the order in all countries where it does not exist.

SEC. 6.   It shall provide a revenue for its support, by charter fees, *per capita* tax on active members of Subordinate

Camps under its jurisdiction, and charges on surplies. It shall have the power to make assessments, when in its judgment the same shall be necessary, by a two-thirds vote of the members present.

SEC. 7. It shall require a semi-annual report from every Subordinate Camp under its jurisdiction and preserve the same.

SEC. 8. It shall hear and determine all appeals and grievances from Subordinate Camps under its jurisdiction, when the same are brought before it in accordance with its laws.

SEC. 9. It shall enact such laws and regulations as may be necessary to enforce its legitimate authority over Subordinate Camps under its control.

SEC. 10. It shall supply a Constitution for the Subordinate Camps.

OBJECTS OF THE ORDER.

SECTION 11. The objects of the order shall be :—

a. To unite Scotchmen, sons of Scotchmen, and their descendants, of good moral character, and possessed of some known reputable means of support, who are over eighteen years of age.

b. To establish a fund for the relief of sick members, and to ameliorate their condition in every reasonable manner.

c. To provide or establish a Beneficiary Fund, from which, on satisfactory evidence of the death of a member, a sum not exceeding one thousand dollars shall be paid, as provided by the Constitution and laws of the Order relative to the Beneficiary Fund.

d. To cultivate fond recollections of Scotland, its customs and amusements.

e. The Camps shall at all times be free from all political and theological sectarianism, and be subject only to the laws of God and of the land in which they respectively exist.

TIME AND PLACE OF ASSEMBLY.

SECTION 12. The Grand Camp shall assemble annually, on the third Tuesday in April, at nine o'clock a.m., at such place as shall have been selected by the vote of a majority of its members present at the next previous annual session, and adjourn its sittings from day to day until its business be completed.

SEC. 13. Special meetings shall be called by the Grand Chief upon the written request of a majority of the representatives to the Grand Camp, representing six or more Subordinate Camps, and the Grand Secretary shall notify by letter each Subordinate Camp entitled to representation in this Grand Camp, also every officer and member of the Grand Camp and also the object of the call.

SEC. 14. This Grand Camp shall be composed of its officers, the representatives from Subordinate Camps, and all Past Grand Chiefs, provided they remain in good standing in their Subordinate Camps.

SEC. 15. This Grand Camp shall not have the power to create a Past Grand Chief. All Grand Chiefs who have served one full, or the balance of an unexpired term, shall be Past Grand Chiefs by virtue of service, and the retiring Grand Chief shall occupy the chair of the Past Grand Chief until his successor is installed.

SEC. 16. Each Subordinate Camp shall be entitled to one Representative in this Grand Camp. Provided, however, that no member shall be eligible as Representative to this Grand Camp unless he has obtained all the degrees of the Order. When the Subordinate Camp has a membership of 100 it shall be entitled to an additional Representative for each additional 100 members or fraction thereof, and such additional Representative and his Alternate shall be elected at the next annual election, after the Camp is entitled thereto.

SEC. 17. At the regular election of Representatives, the Subordinate Camp shall also elect alternates for such Representatives, who shall be recognized as the Alternate Representatives in the event of the inability of the Representatives, or either of them, to attend the annual meeting of the Grand Camp, or of the death or resignation of the Representatives, or either of them, unless the vacancy by death or resignation shall have been filled by said Subordinate Camp ; provided that the Representatives and their Alternates shall not both be admitted during any one annual or special meeting. Any vacancy in the office of Representative or Alternate may be filled by the Snbordinate Camp. An alternate Representative before being admitted to the Grand Camp, shall present, together with his certificate of election, written evidence from the Secretary of Camp, or from the Representative for whom he is elected Alternate, that the Representative is unable to attend the meeting of the Grand Camp.

SEC. 18. A Representative cannot be admitted to this Grand Camp from any Subordinate Camp that is in arrears to the Grand Camp for annual dues, that has neglected to pay the beneficiary or other assessments, make reports of its membership, or is indebted to the Grand Camp for supplies.

SEC. 19. Each officer and member of the Grand Camp shall, at each session thereof attended by him, present to such Grand Camp credentials from his Subordinate Camp showing good standing therein at the last regular meeting of his Camp prior to the session of the Grand Camp.

OFFICERS AND ELECTIONS.

SECTION 20. The Officers of this Grand Camp shall be a Grand Chief, Past Grand Chief, Grand Chieftain, Grand Secretary, Grand Treasurer, Grand Chaplain, Grand Marshal, Grand Standard Bearer, Grand Medical Examiner, Grand Senior Guard, Grand Junior Guard, a Committee on Laws and Appeals of three, a Finance Committee of three, a Committeee on the State of the Order of three, and three Trustees who shall be elected annually, except the Past Grand Chief, provided that no person shall be eligible to the office of Grand Chief who has not been a member of this Grand Camp for one year preceeding his election. The surviving Junior Past Grand Chief shall act as Past Grand Chief.

SEC. 21. The nomination, election and installation of officers shall take place at such time during each annual meeting as the Grand Camp may by resolution provide, but not until the proper order of business is reached as laid down in the Rules of Order for the guidance of this Grand Camp.

SEC. 22. When there is more than one candidate for the same office, it shall require a majority of all the votes cast to elect, and when there are more than two candidates for the same office, the one receiving the least number of votes on each ballot shall be dropped until an election is had.

SEC. 23. During the nomination and election of Officers, no motion, except to take a recess, shall be entertained.

SEC. 24. The Officers (except the Past Grand Chief) of the Grand Camp shall be elected for the term of one year, and until their successors shall be duly installed. The Past Grand Chief shall hold his office from the time of the election and installation of such Officers until the election and installation of their successors in office.

SEC. 25. The election of officers of the Grand Camp shall be by written ballot, and a majority of all ballots cast shall be necessary to a choice.

SEC. 26. Any officer of the Grand Camp may be removed by the Grand Chief for inability to perform the duties of his office, incompetency, inattention to the duties of his office, or conduct unbecoming his position as an officer of the Grand Camp. If the office of any officer becomes vacant by the death, resignation, removal, or otherwise of any officer, the Grand Chief shall appoint from the Past Representative to the Grand Camp a proper and suitable person to such office, to serve as such officer during the remainder of the term in which such appointment shall be made, and the person so appointed and serving shall be entitled to the full honors of the office.

QUORUM.

SECTION 27. Seven members shall constitute a quorum.

SEC. 28. No session of the Grand Camp shall be open for general business unless a quorum be present, but a smaller number may act on the credentials of Representatives, confer the Grand Camp degree, and adjourn from time to time until a quorum be present.

REVENUE.

SECTION 29. The revenue for the Grand Camp shall be :—

Charters and sets of supplies for each Subordinate Camp	$75 00
Benefit Certificates each	1 00
Withdrawal Cards.	25
Rituals	50
Constitutions	5
Applications for membership and Medical Examiner's blanks per 100	1 00

The sales of such further supplies as may be required or the Order and by regulation of the Committee on Supplies, under authority of this Grand Camp.

A per capita tax of fifty cents per annum, payable semi-annually, and chargeable on the 30th day of June, and on the 31st day of December, for each active member of the Order then in good standing ; and such other sources as are in accordance with the objects and business of the Order.

CHARTERS.

SECTION 30. All applications for Charters shall be furnished by the Grand Camp.

SEC. 31. The Grand Chief shall have power to grant Dispensations or Charters during the recess of this Grand Camp and to take such measures as may be necessary to institute Camps where no Camp exists.

SEC. 32. All Subordinate Camps working under dispensations or Charters granted during a recess of this Grand Camp shall be reported at each annual meeting by the Grand Secretary. All Charters shall be countersigned by the Grand Chief and Grand Secretary, with the seal of the Grand Camp affixed.

DUTIES OF OFFICERS.

GRAND CHIEF.

SECTION 33. The Grand Chief shall preside at all meetings of this Grand Camp, and enforce all laws thereof. He shall have the general superintendence of the Order, with power to grant dispensations, when the good of the Order may require it, except for the admission of unqualified persons to membership, or to authorize a violation of law of this Order, or to legalize a wilful violation of such law.

SEC. 34. He shall institute semi-annual pass-words, and with the assistance of the Grand Secretary, he shall furnish the same to each Subordinate Camp in good standing.

SEC. 35. He shall fill all vacancies occasioned by death or otherwise, until an election shall be held. He shall sign all orders on the Grand Treasurer, drawn in accordance with the laws of this Order. He shall sign all documents and papers that require his signature to properly authenticate them.

SEC. 36. At the commencement of each annual meeting he shall appoint a committee of three on credentials ; a committee of three on mileage and per diem ; a committee of three on new business ; and a committee of three on secret work, to serve during such annual meeting.

SEC. 37. At the close of each annual meeting he shall make such appointments of Special Committees as have been provided for ; and he shall have power to fill all vacancies occurring therein during the recess.

SEC. 38. He may appoint District Deputy Grand Chiefs, whenever and wherever he thinks the good of the Order requires.

SEC. 39. He may appoint one or more Deputy Grand Chiefs with power to institute new Camps.

SEC. 40. His correspondence with Subordinate Camps, when practicable, shall be conducted through the Grand Secretary, with the Seal of the Grand Camp attached.

SEC. 41. His decisions upon all questions of law shall be final during a recess of the Grand Camp. He shall report all such decisions to the Grand Camp for approval or rejection.

SEC. 42. He shall submit at the annual meeting of this Grand Camp a printed report of all his official acts during his term of office, and he shall perform such other duties as the laws, rules and usages of the Order require.

SEC. 43. The Grand Chieftain shall preside in the absence of the Grand Chief, and in case of the death, resignation, disqualification, refusal or neglect of the Grand Chief to discharge the duties of his office, he shall then perform all duties incumbent upon the Grand Chief until an election shall be held.

GRAND SECRETARY.

SECTION 44. (1) The Grand Secretary shall keep a correct report of the proceedings of this Grand Camp. He shall read all communications, reports, petitions, etc., and attest all orders drawn on the Grand Treasurer. He shall affix the seal of this Grand Camp to all official documents. He shall prepare for publication a copy of the proceedings of this Camp within one month after the close of each annual or called meeting. He shall also make to this Grand Camp on the first day of each annual meeting, a complete printed statement of the condition of this Order.

(2) He shall complete and arrange for publication, subject to the approval of the Committee on Laws, all amendments to the Constitution and Laws adopted by the Grand Camp.

(3) In the months of June and December of each year he shall furnish the semi-annual password, as prepared by the Grand Chief, to the several Chiefs of Subordinate Camps.

(4) He shall promptly perform all duties relating to the Beneficiary Fund, according to the provisions and require-ents of the Constitution and Laws of this Order.

(5) He shall draw and attest all orders (which must also efore payment be signed by the Grand Chief) for payment of eneficiary and for payment of bills that have been approved y the Finance Committee. All orders so drawn, attested, nd signed shall be paid by the Grand Treasurer on demand, r as soon as possible thereafter.

(6) On satisfactory proof furnished to the Grand Camp of he death of a member, he shall give notice to each and every ubordinate Camp of the death of such member, with a state-ment of the following particulars, viz. : the name of such deceased member, name of the Camp to which he belonged, date of initiation into the Order, residence, age, death, place and cause of death ; and if any reason be assigned by the Grand Secretary, the Grand Camp or by the Subordinate Camp of which such deceased brother was a member, why the beneficiary on account of such death should not be paid, then a full statement of the grounds thereof. He shall also state the amount collected for and paid as Beneficiary on account of the death of the member, who died next previous to the death of the member on account of whose death such notice shall be given, when and to whom paid, with the number of the assess-ment for such Beneficiary, and if not paid he shall state the reason therefor ; and if paid after such notice, he shall when paid make such statement. He shall also, in and by such notice, request each and every Subordinate Camp to forward to him the last assessment, as required or shall hereafter be required by the Laws of the Order ; and, if an assessment be necessary, he shall also at the same time furnish to each and every Subordinate Camp advance Beneficiary assessment blanks and Camp assessment notices, with blank receipts thereon, as and in the form and for the purposes required or shall hereafter be required and by the Beneficiary Laws of the

Order, adopted by the Grand Camp.

(7) He shall conduct the correspondence of the Grand Camp.

(8) He shall keep a record of the name, number, date of institution, names of officers, and the location of all Subordinate Camps. He shall keep a full record of each member initiated into the Order, with date, place of birth, nativity or descent, age, occupation, residence, and of the beneficiary or beneficiaries of such member as furnished him by the Camp of such member, also a list of all members expelled or suspended.

(9) He shall have charge of the seal, books, papers, medical examination forms sent to him by the Grand Physician, and all private work belonging to the Grand Camp, except the books and papers of the Grand Treasurer.

(10) He shall deliver to the Grand Camp, or to his successor in office, all property, books, and papers of the Grand Camp and of the Order in his charge or possession at the expiration of his term of office.

(11) He shall keep a true and correct account between this Grand Camp and all Subordinate Camps. He shall present to the Grand Camp on the first day of each annual meeting, a full and correct statement of the amount of money received and disbursed during the year, and for what purposes.

(12) He shall receive all money due the Graud Camp and shall deposit the same. weekly, to the credit of the Grand Camp, in a Chartered Bank to be selected by the Grand Camp, and shall send a duplicate deposit receipt to the Grand Treasurer showing the amount of the last deposit and the several funds to which it belongs.

(13) He shall issue to the several Camps semi-annually, circulars showing the receipts of and for, and expenditures from, the General Fund, in detail, and a correct statement of the Beneficiary Fund as appearing and as should appear by the books of his office.

(14) He shall perform such other duties as the laws and usages of this Order require, and may from time to time appoint and discharge such assistants as shall be provided to him by the Grand Camp, and he shall be responsible for the acts of such assistants in the transaction of the business of his office.

(15) Before entering upon the discharge of his duties as

such Grand Secretary, he shall give a good and sufficient bond, from a responsible Canadian Guarantee Company, at the expense of the Grand Camp, for the faithful performance of his duties as such Grand Secretary, in the penal sum of not less than $1000, which bond must be approved by the Grand Camp, or during the interim of sessions, by, and deposited with, the Grand Chief ; and for his services he shall receive such sum as the Grand Camp may determine.

GRAND TREASURER.

SECTION 45. (1) The Grand Treasurer shall perform all duties relating to the Beneficiary Fund, as prescribed in and by the Constitution and laws of the Order.

(2) He shall countersign all orders drawn on him, in accordance with the Constitution and laws of this Order. He shall keep a correct and seperate account of all money deposited to the credit of this Grand Camp, and paid by him on account of the Beneficiary Fund, and only pay out the same, on orders duly drawn on him to pay Beneficiary Certificates. The Beneficiary Fund shall not be used for any other purposes. He shall also keep a correct and separate account of all money deposited to the credit of and paid out from the General Fund. The General Fund shall not be used to pay Beneficiary Certificates.

(3) At the commencement of each quarter he shall transmit to the Grand Chief, Grand Secretary, and each member of the Finance Committee, a statement comprising the following items :—

General Fund.—Balance on hand at last report, total receipts and payments,, and balance on hand.

Beneficiary Fund.—Balance on hand at last report, total received for each assessment, total disbursements, and balance on hand at the commencement of each quarter.

(4) He shall have his accounts correctly posted, and ready for examination by the Finance Committee, immediately after the close of each fiscal year, and at such other times as they shall require and demand : and he shall make to the Grand Camp, on the first day of its annual meeting, a full and correct printed report of the financial affairs of the Grand

Camp, of all matters and things done, and of all money received, paid, and delivered by him as Grand Treasurer during his term of office ; the condition of the several funds, the balances then on hand, and the state of the Treasury of the Grand Camp at the time of such report.

(5) He shall deliver to the Grand Camp or its proper officer, whenever called upon to do so by the Grand Chief or Finance Committee, all money, papers, and other property in his hands, or under his charge belonging to the Order.

(6) For the faithful performance and discharge of his duties as such Grand Treasurer he shall receive such sum as the Grand Camp may determine.

GRAND PHYSICIAN.

SECTION 46. The Grand Physician shall examine all certificates of examination sent by the Examining Physician of each Subordinate Camp, write thereon his approval or disapproval of the same, and forward them to the Grand Secretary, who shall notify the said Subordinate Camp. If the examination and recommendation of the Physician of the Subordinate Camp be disapproved by the Grand Physician the applicant shall not be eligible to membership entitling him to participation in the Beneficiary Fund, or to sick benefits in said Camp.

If the Grand Physician shall approve, the applicant named therein shall be deemed eligible to membership so far as physical qualifications and conditions are concerned.

It shall also be his duty to prepare forms of examination for the guidance of the Subordinate Camps, medical proof papers, to be filled up on the death of a member, and other duties as determined by the Grand Camp ; he shall be a legally qualified practitionar, must be a member in good standing in the Order, and, by virtue of his office, shall be a member of the Grand Camp. In no case can he hold the office of physician to a Subordinate Camp while acting as Grand Medical Examiner. He shall be compensated for his services out of the general fund, as Grand Camp may determine.

GRAND CHAPLAIN.

SECTION 47. The Grand Chaplain shall offer invocations to, and ask blessings of, the Deity, and perform such other duties as are required by the Laws, Rules, and Usages of this Order.

OTHER GRAND CAMP OFFICERS.

SECTION 48. The immediate Past Grand Chief, Grand Marshal, Grand Senior Guard, and Grand Junior Guard, shall perform all the duties required of them at their several stations in this Grand Camp, such as are traditionally appropriate to their respective stations, or as may be assigned to them respectively by the Grand Camp.

COMMITTEES.

SECTION 49. The following committees, each consisting of three members, shall be appointed by the Grand Chief at every regular session, viz. : 1. Credentials and Returns ; 2, Mileage and Per Diem. The Committee on Mileage and Per Diem shall be composed only of Representatives.

SEC. 50. The Grand Chief, Grand Chieftain and Grand Secretary shall constitute a Committe on Supplies. They shall contract for all needed supplies and printing, in accordance with such resolutions or regulations as have been or shall be adopted by the Grand Camp, and shall fix the price of all supplies, except in cases where the prices have been fixed by the Grand Camp. They shall present a printed report, in detail, of their proceedings and doings to the Grand Camp at each annual meeting.

SEC. 51. It shall be the duty of the Finance Committee to examine all bills, and to approve the same if correct in every particular ; to return all disapproved bills, with the reasons for disapproval, to the Grand Secretary, who shall refer the same to the Grand Chief ; to examine the Grand Secretary's books ; to examine the returns from all Subordinate Camps, together with the abstract reports of the Grand Secretary as presented at each annual meeting ; to examine the Grand Treasurer's books and vouchers, and to submit a printed re port of the finances of the Grand Camp and Order, and also as to the correctness of said returns and reports, at each annual meeting.   They shall also submit to the Grand Camp at each annual meeting, estimates in detail of the receipts and expenses for the twelve months ending the thirty-first day of December in each year.   They shall keep a record in a book, to be furnished by the Grand Secretary, of the date payee, object, amount and date of approval of each account approved by them.   They shall make special examinations of the books and accounts of the Grand Treasurer and Grand Secretary when directed by the Grand Chief.   They shall also perform such other duties as the Grand Camp may from time to time direct.

SEC. 52. The Committee on Laws and Appeals shall examine and approve the By-laws of all Subordinate Camps, and all subsequent amendments or alterations made thereto, provided the same do not repeat or conflict with the Constitution or Laws of this Grand Camp, and such By-laws shall not take effect until so approved.   They shall examine and report upon all proposed amendments to the Constitution and Laws of this Grand Camp.   They shall also examine all appeals and grievances that may arise in this Grand Camp, together with all appeals and grievances that may be taken from a Subordinate Camp to this Grand Camp, or between individual members thereof, that may be referred to them in accordance with the laws of this Order.   They shall not receive new testimony, but shall base their decision upon the evidence furnished, and report to this body for approval or rejection, or to the Grand Chief during a recess.   They shall make a written report to this Grand Camp at each annual meeting.

SEC. 53. The Committee on the State of the Order shall report to the Grand Chief their recommendations on all matters referred to them, by him, during the recess of the Grand Camp, and to the Grand Camp on all matters referred to them at each annual meeting.

SEC. 54. The Committee on Credentials shall examine the credentials of all Representatives to this Grand Camp.

SEC. 55. The Committee on Mileage and Per Diem shall make up and present to the Grand Camp, and have ready for use by the afternoon session of the last day of each annual, or special, meeting, duplicate pay rolls, whereon shall be recorded the name, residence, number of miles travelled, by the most direct trunk line or route, and the amount due each member for mileage and per diem.

SEC. 56. Other Committees that may be created from time to time, shall at each meeting examine and report on such matters as may be referred to them.

SEC. 57. All formal action by the Grand Trustees and Standing Committees during the recess of the Grand Camp shall be in writing, signed by a majority, and shall be forwarded to the Grand Secretary, who shall record the same in books kept for that purpose.

MILEAGE AND PER DIEM.

SECTION 58. This Grand Camp shall pay mileage to its members and representatives from Subordinate Camps, who may be in attendance at its session, at the rate of three cents per mile each way, from the place of their residence.

SEC. 59. Per Diem shall be paid to each member as the Grand Camp, while in session, may direct.

ORDER OF BUSINESS.

SECTION 60. When the presiding officer takes the chair the officers and members shall take their respective seats, and at the sound of the gavel there shall be general silence.

SEC. 61. Business at the annual meetings shall be taken up daily, in the following order :—

1. Calling Roll of Officers.
2. Reading Minutes.
3. Report of Committee on Credentials.
4 Reports of Officers.
5. Reports of Committees in the following order : Finance ; Laws and Appeals ; State of the Order ; Mileage and Per Diem ; Secret Work.
6. Reports of Special Committees.
7. Unfinished Business.
8. New Business.
9. Nomination and Election of Officers.
10. Installation.
11. Closing.

SEC. 62. This Order of business may be transposed at any time as occasion may require. All petitions, resolutions and communications from Subordinate Camps, or from any member of the Order, shall be endorsed by a member of the Grand Camp and presented to the Grand Secretary, who shall, without delay, read its title or such portion of the paper as may be necessary, when it shall be referred to the appropriate Committee without debate.

SEC. 63. No motion to alter, amend, or add to the Constitution shall be entertained, unless a notice in writing, stating the proposed alteration, amendment or addition, shall have been given on or before the 1st day of December to the Grand Secretary, who shall send a copy of such notice or notices of motion to all Subordinate Camps, and all members of the Grand Camp, for their consideration, and the motion can only be carried by receiving two-thirds of the votes present.

RETURNS.

SECTION 64. Each Subordinate Camp, working under the immediate jurisdiction of the Grand Camp, shall make out semi-annual returns of its work and business to the Grand Secretary, up to and including the 30th day of June and the 31st day of December in each year; and shall forward such returns, together with the *per capita* tax, to the Grand Secretary, within thirty days after such dates respectively; and, in case it fails so to do. such Subordinate Camp shall not be entitled to representation at the next ensuing session of the Grand Camp, except for good cause the Grand Camp shall deem it proper to allow such representation. The Grand Secretary shall supply all Subordinate Camps with forms on which to make the above returns on or before the first days of June and December in each year.

BENEFICIARY FUND.

SECTION 65. Upon the death of an active member of the Order, who has not failed to pay within the prescribed thirty days, the last preceding assessment, or is not six months in arrears for dues, there shall be a payment from the Order not exceeding one thousand dollars ($1,000), raised by *per capita* assessment by the Subordinate Camps and paid over to the Grand Camp, and by the Grand Camp through the Chief of the Subordinate Camp of which the deceased brother was a member, and by him paid over to the beneficiary or benefic· iaries of such deceased brother as provided by and subject to the provisions of the Constitution and the Beneficiary Laws of the Order. Such fund shall be managed and controlled by the Grand Camp.

BENEFICIARY CERTIFICATES.

SECTION 66. Every Subordinate Camp shall forward to the Grand Secretary, all applications for membership, within six days after the applicant is initiated, and with each application one dollar to pay for a beneficiary certificate, which shall be issued to him by the Grand Camp and returned to the Chief, who shall countersign the same and deliver it to him.

SEC. 67. Each applicant shall direct in his application to whom he desires his beneficiary paid. The beneficiary or beneficiaries may thereafter be changed, as provided in the Beneficiary Laws of the Order.

SEC. 68. A beneficiary certificate of a member shall not be changed, or a new one issued, until the surrender of the original, except that when a beneficiary certificate is lost or destroyed, a written statement of the brother that such cer· tificate has been lost or destroyed, with the facts thereof, a certificate of the Chief of his Camp that such brother has paid his beneficiary assessments, is not six months in arrears for dues, is worthy of belief, and that he believes such statement to be true, attested by the Secretary with the seal of the Camp, shall be received in place of such original certificate, and a duplicate or new certificate shall be issued thereon. The fee for such duplicate certificate shall be fifty cents.

REGALIA.

SECTION 69. The regalia of the Grand and Subordinate Camps shall be such as prescribed by the Grand Camp, or adopted and approved from time to time, at an annual session of the Grand Camp.

SEC. 70. The regalia of the Grand Camp shall be the Grand Camp tartan, and no brother shall be allowed to wear such regalia, except such as may have had the Grand Camp degree conferred upon them. The Balmoral Bonnet shall be the regulation or standard Bonnet of the Grand Camp.

PASSWORDS AND CIRCULARS.

SECTION 71. The Grand Chief shall have the exclusive right of creating and promulgating all passwords, to call in and change the same when necessary, and prescribe their application and use.

SEC. 72. No circular, resolution, or document relating to the ritual, laws, or general management of this Order, shall be issued or circulated by any Subordinate Camp or, member of the Order, or be read in or acted upon by any Subordinate Camp, unless the same shall bear the approval of the Grand Chief, or be circulated under the immediate jurisdiction of the Grand Camp, unless it bears the approval of the Grand Chief.

Provided, however, that nothing in this section shall prevent the discussion of proposed alterations in the Constitution or Ritual, but all documents in reference to such proposed alterations, which are intended for circulation in Subordinate Camps, must first be referred to the Grand Chief.

SEAL.

SEC. 73. Every Camp shall provide itself with a seal, with appropriate devices, and such seal shall be affixel to all its official documents. With the approval of the Grand Camp it may change its seal or adopt a new seal, when deemed by it proper.

FORMATION OF SUBORDINATE CAMPS.

SECTION 74. Subordinate Camps exist by virtue of charters from the Grand Camp.

SEC. 75. The Constitution of Subordinate Camps shall be such, as is, or shall be prescribed by the Grand Camp.

SEC. 76. A Subordinate Camp shall be composed of not less

han fifteen Beneficiary members at its institution, and after-
ards of not less than nine Beneficiary members, and shall
ld stated meetings at least monthly.

SEC. 77 The officers of a Subordinate Camp shall be elected by written ballot. Their term of office shall be for one
year, and until their successors shall be duly elected and in-
talled.

APPLICATION FOR CHARTER OF A SUBORDINATE CAMP.

SECTION 78. If the Applicants for a charter for a Subordinate Camp be within the jurisdiction of the Grand Camp,
and desirous of coming under the jurisdiction of said Grand
Camp, the application will be addressed—

To the Grand Chief, Officers, and Members of the Grand Camp
of the Sons of Scotland Benevolent Society :

We, the undersigned, respectfully apply to your honorable
body for a Charter of a Subordinate Camp, to be called————
Camp, to work under the laws of the Order.

(Signed)
This petition shall be signed by at least fifteen persons, and
accompanied by a fee of seventy-five dollars.

CONSTITUTION OF SUBORDINATE CAMPS

OF

THE SONS OF SCOTLAND

BENEVOLENT SOCIETY.

COMPOSITION, POWERS, AND NAME.

SECTION 1.   This Camp shall consist of not less than fifteen Beneficiary members at the institution thereof, having the requisite qualifications, and shall possess all the powers and privileges of a Subordinate Camp, by virtue of a charter, duly granted by the Grand Camp, under whose authority it shall exist while acting in conformity with the Constitution, laws, rules, and regulations of the said Grand Camp.

SEC 2.   This Camp shall be known as————— Camp Sons of Scotland Benevolent Society, and it shall be designated by a number according to seniority of its organization.

SEC. 3.   The name of the Camp shall be associated with the history, poetry, or romance of Scotland, and chosen by written ballot.   A majority of all ballots cast shall be necessary to a choice.   No two Subordinate Camps shall have the same name in the same jurisdiction.

SEC. 4.   No camp shall come into existence in any city or town, where a Camp is already established, without the consent of the Camp or Camps already in existence in such city or town.   Provided, that when a Camp objects to the formation of a new Camp, the Grand Chief, may, if in his opinion the good of the Order requires it, overrule the objection and grant a dispensation.

MEETINGS AND QUORUM.

SECTION 5. Every Subordinate Camp shall hold its regular meetings at least monthly. and at the place designated in its charter.

SEC. 6. Five members shall constitute a quorum, and all meetings shall be opened and closed in conformity with the Ritual of the Order.

SEC. 7. The Chief shall call a special meeting on the death of a member, and shall call other special meetings on the written request of seven members in good standing in the Camp, and he may at any time, when he deems it for the best interests of his Camp, call a special meeting thereof. Every call for a special meeting shall specify the object of the meeting, and no other business shall be transacted there it. Notice of any special meeting may be given to the brethern personally, or by at least one day's previous notice, by letter deposited in the post-office, addressed to them respectively at their last known respective places of residence, or by publication in a news-paper, when not revealing any matters that should be held in the secrecy of the Camp.

SEC. 8. No appropriation of money, unless it be the business for which the special meeting was called, no balloting for members, and no applications for membership can be had at any spec al meeting of a Camp.

SEC. 9. The Chief of a Camp, when present shall preside, and the Chieftain shall act in his absence, and cannot depute any other brother to perform that duty. In case of the temporary absence of any officer from a meeting, the Chief, or the Chieftain, acting as chairman in the absence of the Chief, shall appoint some suitable brother to fill the chair or position of such absent officer, during such temporary absence, but such appointment shall not extend beyond such temporary absence or such meeting.

The Chief may call a Past Chief to fill his chair during initiation.

Should both Chief and Chieftain be absent from any regular meeting, any active member who is in good standing may be chosen to preside by a majority of the brethern present.

MEMBERSHIP.

SECTION. 10. To become an active member of a Subordin-ate Camp the applicant must be Scotch, of Scotch parentage, or of Scotch descent. He must be of good moral character, possessed of some reputable means of support, free from dis-ease, not under eighteen years nor over fifty years of age at the time of his initiation.

Persons who pass the medical examination, and pay full yearly dues and all assessments, shall be entitled to sick and funeral benefits, and the benefit of the Beneficiary Fund.

Persons over fifty years of age, and applicants who fail to pass successfully the medical examination required by the Order, may be admitted as honorary members under restrictions.

SEC. 11. A petition for membership must be signed by the applicant, with the recommendation of two members of the Camp in good standing indorsed thereon.

There must be presented with every such petition the in-itiation fee, or so much thereof, not less than two dollars as the By-Laws of the Camp shall prescribe. At or before the time of initiation of any such applicant, he shall pay to the Camp the balance of his initiation fee, if any, then remaining unpaid, together with one advance Beneficiary assessment, and such dues, not exceeding three months dues, as the By-Laws now or hereafter shall prescribe.   The application shall be read at a stated meeting of the Subordinate Camp at least two weeks previous to ballot, and in no case shall this be dis-pensed with, except in the institution of Subordinate Camps ; and then only by dispensation from the Grand Chief or one of his Deputies.

SEC. 12. An applicant for active membership shall not be admitted, unless on being examined by the Examining Phys-ician—who shall be a licentiate of a regular school of medi-cine,—he shall be found of sound mind and body, and have the qualifications required in the formula prescribed by the Grand Camp, and the certificate of the Examining Physician shall first have been approved, in writing by the Grand Phys-ician.

SEC. 13. Upon the presentation of a petition in proper

form, accompanied by the initiation fee, or such part thereof, not less than two dollars, as provided by the By-laws of the Camp, the Chief shall, without motion, appoint a committee of three, none of whom shall have recommended him, whose duty it shall be to enquire into the qualifications and char‑ acter of the applicant for membership, and in two weeks from their appointment, unless further time be granted by the Chief or Camp, the committee shall make a written report, recommending either an acceptance or rejection of the peti‑ tion.

SEC. 14. Upon the report of the Committee, if favorable, the applicant shall be balloted for. If two or more black balls appear (and in order that no rejection be had by reason of having black balls cast by mistake) the Chief, without stating the result of the vote, shall immediately order a new ballot, and if again two or more black balls appear he shall declare the candidate rejected, and no petition shall be received by any Subordinate Camp from a person who has been rejected in that or any other Camp, until the expiration of six months after such rejection. In every case of an applicant being rejected his initiation fee shall be returned to him.

SEC. 15. A brother's membership shall commence at the time of his initiation, or, if a member of another Camp, at the time of his election and admission as a member of the Camp with which he has deposited his card. The candidate must, if elected, come forward for initiation within one month, unless prevented by some unavoidable cause. If not initiated within one month the Camp may demand a re-examination by the physicians. If the candidate is delayed six months he shall be re-examined. If a person is proposed and elected, and previous to initiation the Camp find he is not a fit person to become a member, it may refuse, by a majority vote of the brethren present, to initiate him and in that case it shall refund him his money.

SEC. 16. Good standing of a member shall mean one who is a contributing member of the Camp ; who is not suspended for failure to pay his Beneficiary assessments ; is not six months in arrear for dues ; and against whom no charge of delinquency or misconduct is pending.

SEC. 17. Membership is defined as follows :—

Active Members.—All above eighteen years and under fifty years of age at the time of their initiation, respectively, who have passed the medical examination.

Honorary Members.—Those over fifty years of age at the time of their respective initiations ; those who have failed to pass the medical examination, and have been elected such honorary members. Honorary members shall be entitled to speak and vote on all questions appertaining to the business of their respective Camps, but shall not vote on any question of finance. They shall pay annually, such dues as the By-Laws of the Camp may determine.

OFFICERS.

SECTION 18. The officers of a Subordinate Camp shall be a Chief, Chieftain, Past Chief, Chaplain, Secretary. Financial Secretary, Treasurer, Marshal, Standard Bearer, Senior Guard and Junior Guard, who shall be elected annually, at the last meeting in December. There shall also be elected at the same time an Examining Physician and three trustees, and a Piper or Pipers (if such there be among the brethren), who shall serve for one year.

SEC. 19. Any active member in good standing and having taken the degrees shall be eligible to any office in the Camp, except that of Chief, but no brother shall hold two offices at one time, except in the case of trustees, who shall be neither the Secretary, Financial Secretary, nor Treasurer. To qualify for the office of Chief the brother must have all the degrees and served one full term in a subordinate office, except at the institution of a Camp.

SEC. 20. Nominations and elections shall take place in the order named in Section 18. The voting shall be by written ballot, and a majority of all ballots cast shall be necessary to elect.

SEC. 21. The officers of the Camp legally elected, if duly qualified, shall be installed at the first stated meeting in January, by the Grand Chief or his deputy, where there are such, or by the senior Active Past Chief of the Camp present at the meeting of the Camp. If a member, who has been elected, fail to present himself for installation, unless prevented by sickness or other unavoidable cause, the Chief of the Camp may declare the office vacant, and order a new election to be held forthwith to fill the vacancy. No member one month in arrears for dues, or owing for one Beneficiary assessment for thirty days, shall be installed into any office of the Camp, nor shall any officer who has been installed, retain his seat after he shall become and be two months in arrears for dues, or has failed to pay his beneficiary assessment.

Sec. 22. Any officer, after due trial, may be removed for inability, incompetency, inattention to the duties of his office, or conduct unbecoming a member, by a majority vote of the brethern present at a regular meeting ; and vacancies occur-ing by death, resignation, or otherwise shall be filled in the manner of the original selection.

DUTIES OF OFFICERS.

Section 23 The Chief shall exercise all the rights and perform all the duties appertaining to his office. He shall have a watchful care over his Camp and see that the consti-tutional enactments, rules, and edicts of the Grand Camp and the Constitution of the Order, so far as they apply to Subor-dinate Camps and members thereof ; and the rules, regula-tions, and By-Laws of the Subordinate Camp are duly and promptly observed, and that the work and business of the Camp be carried out properly and uniformly. He shall cause to be executed and securely preserve and keep the official bonds and securities of the Trustees and Secretary. He shall preserve strict order and decorum, and decide all questions of order, and any member may appeal from his decision to the Camp. He shall not be entitled to vote, except when electing officers, balloting for candidates, and when the members are equally divided on other questions. He shall inspect all ballots on applications for membership, and after examination of same. by the Chieftain and Marshal, report thereon to the Camp. He shall sign all orders drawn on the Treasurer for the payment of such sums of money as may from time to time be voted by the Camp, and also such documents as may require his signa-, ture to authenticate them. He shall appoint standing and all other committees as may be required by the Constitution

and By-Laws, or by direction of the Camp.   He shall appoint
a committee to visit sick members, and cause weekly benefits
to be paid to them if entitled thereto.   Upon the death of a
brother in good standing he shall cause funeral benefits to be
paid, and ascertain from their family or friends their wishes
regarding the funeral.

SEC. 24.   The Chieftain shall assist the Chief in all his
duties and in preserving order and decorum in the Camps,
preside over the Camp in his absence, and at all other times,
perform such duties as may be assigned him by the Camp, or
the Chief thereof.

SEC. 25.   The Chaplain shall open and close the Camp
with prayer, and perform all other obligatory ceremonials as
prescribed in the Ritual of the Camp, and such other duties
as comport with his office of Chaplain.

SEC. 26.   The Secretary shall keep a true and perfect
record of the proceedings of the Camp, write a l communications, fill up all documents and certificates granted by the
Camp, and issue all notices required either for regular or
special meetings.   He shall make out the semi-annual
reports of the work and business of the Camp, properly
signed and attested, with the seal of the Camp attached.
He shall give immediate notice to each Camp in the same
Town or City of any petition for membership, and the names
of the Committee to whom the petition was referred, notify
such Camp or Camps of all rejections and suspension of members, with cause and date thereof, keep a record of same, and
of every similar notice received from any other Camp, setting
forth the date and cause of same.   He shall also, when a
member is admitted to membership in his Camp by card, immediately notify the Camp granting the card, giving the date
of admission.   He shall keep a record of the names of the
members of the Camp, their ages, occupations, and residences,
and their standing, respectively, noting from time to time in
a marginal column, the death. suspension, expulsion, resignation, or withdrawal of any member, with the date thereof.
He shall, within six days of the initiation of a candidate for
ward to the Grand Secretary the application for membership
of such candidate, with the fee for Beneficiary Certificate.
He shall at once notify the Grand Secretary, of all withdrawals,
suspensions, expulsions, or reinstatements in his Camp, giving

the name and number of the Beneficiary Certificate in each case. He shall perform such other duties as the Constitution, laws, and customs of the Order may require of him, and shall, upon the installation of his successor in office, deliver up to him the seal, books and papers in his possession, belonging to the Camp and the Order.

SEC. 27. The Financial Secretary shall keep the accounts of the Camp and of its members, receive all money due the Camp, and immediately pay the same over to the Treasurer, taking his receipt therefor. He shall prepare a semi-annual report to the Grand Camp, which report, having been approved, signed by the proper officers, and a copy of same kept as a record, shall be forwarded to the Grand Secretary within one week of such approval. He shall attest all orders drawn on the Treasurer for benefits by Visiting Committees of the Camp, or for money directed to be paid at regular meetings, and no others. He shall read out in regular meetings of the Camp the names of members in arrear for three months dues and over, specify the amount due the Camp, and, when any member becomes suspended for non-payment of dues, note such fact, with date thereof, on the account of such member. He shall attend committees appointed to audit the books and accounts of the Camp, and render such assistance as may be necessary. He shall deliver up to his successor, at the end of his official term, all books. moneys, papers, etc., appertaining to his office, to the Camp and to the Order, not already delivered over to the Camp, and generally discharge such other duties as may be required of him by the Camp and laws and customs of the Order, and give such bond before entering on the duties of his office as the Camp shall require.

SEC. 28. The Treasurer shall receive from the Financial Secretary all money for the use of the Camp, give his receipt therefor, and pay all orders when signed by the Chief and attested by the financial Secretary. He shall have his books ready for settlement at the expiration of his term, or for examination by a duly appointed Auditing Committee, at any time, when required by the Camp, and attend committees for that purpose. He shall also give a quarterly statement of its funds, and furnish the Camp, at the last meeting in the term, with a report of receipts and expenditures for the term, supported by vouchers. He shall deliver to his successor, at the expiration of his term of office, all moneys remaining in his hands, and all books and papers appertaining thereto and to his office, and belonging to the Camp or this Order, to which the Camp shall be entitled, and give such bond before entering on the duties of his office as the Camp shall require, with sureties, subject to approval by the Camp.

Sec. 29. The Marshal shall have charge of the regalia and other property of the Camp intrusted to his care, and shall perform such other duties as pertain to his office.

Sec. 30. The Standard Bearer, Senior Guard and Junior Guard shall perform such duties as are appropriate to their respective offices, or as may be assigned them by the Chief.

Sec. 31. The Examining Physician shall examine candidates for active membership, as to their freedom from disease and disability. He shall use the form prescribed by the Grand Camp, and such examination shall embrace all questions and all matters mentioned and referred to in such form, and for the faithful performance of this duty he shall receive such compensation as may be provided by the By-Laws of the Camp.

Sec. 32. The Trustees shall have general supervision of all the property of the Camp. They shall invest, in such savings bank or securities as the Camp shall direct, such sums as it shall order to be drawn from the Treasury for that purpose. They shall have the custody of all securities of the Camp for money loaned or invested. They shall collect or realize all such sums, when so directed by the Camp, and shall collect all interest, rents, or other money or claims arising from such investments belonging to the Camp or to which it shall be entitled, and pay the money collected by them to the Financial Secretary. On the last stated meeting in June and December they shall report their transactions to the Camp, and they shall make an inventory of its property, and produce and report the same at such meeting. They shall receive, and securely keep, the official bonds of, and securities given by, the Financial Secretary and Treasurer. Before entering upon the duties of their office they shall give bonds with approved sureties or security, and in such penal sum as the Camp may require, for the faithful performance and discharge of their duties as Trustees.

COMMITTEES.

SECTION 33. Every newly elected Chief shall appoint a committee of not less than five members for the ensuing term, which shall be known as the Amusement Committee, whose duties shall be to bring before the Camp propositions for entertainments, and, with the Chief, have the charge and management of any such entertainments when held.

SEC. 34. The Chief shall appoint a Standing Committee on Rules, to whom shall be referred all amendments thereto, all proposed rules, and all questions of order not otherwise disposed of.

SEC. 35. The Chief shall appoint such other committees as may be necessary for the speedy and effectual transaction of Camp business, and a prompt attendance to their duties shall be required by the Chief and by the Camp.

For a violation or neglect of duty by any such committee, or any member thereof, the Camp may impose and enforce such punishment (consistent with the gravity of the offence) as permitted by sections 68 to 72 inclusive of this Constitution, and the proceedings in any such matter shall be the same as for the trial of offences by members for the violation of the laws of the Order, as provided by this Constitution.

REPRESENTATIVES TO GRAND CAMP.

SECTION 36. Every Subordinate Camp shall annually elect to the Grand Camp one Representative for the first one hundred or less number of active members comprising the Camp, and if there be more than one hundred active members, then one Representative for each additional one hundred members, or fractional part thereof.

FEES AND DUES.

SECTION 37. The fees for initation, degrees and reinstatement shall be such as the By-Laws of the Camp now or hereafter shall provide; but in no case shall they be less than eight dollars for initiation, and degrees and three dollars for reinstatement.

Sec. 38. Each active member of every Camp shall pay into the Treasury thereof, as regular dues, not less than three dollars per annum. All regular dues from its members to any Subordinate Camp, shall be payable from time to time in advance, and at equal stated periods, as now or hereafter shall be provided by any such Camp by its By-Laws, in p r-suance of the provisions of this article.

Sec. 39. If the funds of any Subordinate Camp become exhausted, each active member of the Camp shall make such contribution to relieve brethren entitled to weekly benefits under its By-Laws and this Constitution as shall be determined by two-thirds of the members present and voting at a regular meeting of the Camp ; but such determination shall not be made at the same meeting at which the proposal or motion to raise or make such contributions shall be made. No active member present at the time such a motion shall be before the Camp shall be excused from voting thereon.

Non-Payment of Dues.

Section 40. If any active member of a Camp shall be three months in arrear for dues, he shall forfeit all right to, and stand suspended f om, all funeral and sick benefits as follows, namely : If he shall be three months and less than six months in arrear for dues then from the expiration of such three months to the time of payment, and for one month after such payment ; if he shall be six months and less than nine months in arrear for dues, such suspension shall continue until the payment of such six months' dues, and for two months after such payment ; if he shall be nine months and less than twelve months in arrear for dues, such suspension shall continue until the payment of such nine months' dues, and for three months after the payment ; and if he shall be in arrear twelve months for dues, the Financial Secretary shall report that fact to the Camp, and the member so in arrear twelve months shall be dropped from the membership of the Camp, shall cease to be a member of the Order, shall stand suspended from all rights and privileges until restored, and, if restored, shall not be entitled to any benefits or privileges for or during any part of the six months next following such restoration.

If, however, such member be at the time of such suspension under charges for a violation of any of the laws of the Order, then, notwithstanding such suspension, before any restoration can be made such proceeding shall be at the option of the Camp as provided by Sections 68 to 72 inclusive of this Constitution ; and, if such m mber be found guilty, his punishment shall be determined and imposed, at the option of the Camp, in the manner and form and with like proceedings as provided in said Sections, and without regard or reference to such suspension or the result thereof.

If a member die six months in arrear for dues, no Beneficiary shall be paid on account of the death of such member, and no one shall be entitled to receive any beneficiary by reason of his death.

This section shall not include Beneficiary assessmen's as dues.

SEC. 41. A brother who is suspended from his Camp for an amount equal to twelve months' dues, and who appeals to be reinstated, shall make application in the same manner and be subject to the same investigation, medical examination, and ballot as if he had applied for initiation, and shall pay such fees for reinstatement as are required by the By-Laws of the Camp in the case of application for, and initiation to membership in the Camp ; this shall also apply to any member suspended from the Camp, for other causes than the non-payment of dues.

SEC. 42. Payment of dues and arrears during sickness of a member in arrear shall not entitle him to weekly benefits during such sickness, nor funeral benefits should death result therefrom. But should he die, and his means be not sufficient to provide decent interment, the Camp may take special steps in the case.

SEC. 43. Reinstatement to weekly benefits, by virtue of payment shall date from the entire recovery from the sickness during the existence of which such payment is made ; but in no case shall such recovery qualify him to receive benefits until the expiration of the term, for which he was suspended from benefits, by the provisions of the foregoing sections of this article.

SEC. 44. Arrears for dues, when a brother is not under actual suspension from membership therefor by the operation

of section 40, shall not exclude any such member from visita-
tion, care, and attention during sickness and disability, but
the same shall be bestowed upon him as in other case.

Sec. 45. Subordinate Camps are hereby allowed to retain
in their Camp, without paying dues, any aged or infirm
brother, w ose circumstances justify the same, who has been
in good standing in any Camp for not less than ten years.

Benefits.

Section 46. Every brother in good standing who shall be
rendered incapable, by sickness, accident, or injury to his
person, of following any business, vocation, or employment,
whereby he may obtain a livelihood—provided such sickness
or injury shall not have been occasioned by intemperance or
immoral conduct—shall be entitled to receive from the funds
of the Camp, such sum per week, and for such length of time
as its By-Laws may prescribe.

Sec. 47. Any brother being taken sick must notify the
Secretary of his Camp immediately and furnish such proofs of
inability to work and at such times as its By-Laws prescribe.
Any brother taken sick when absent from his usual place of
residence must notify his Camp immediately and furnish to
the Secretary of his Camp the necessary or proper certificate
of a physician as to his sickness and physical condition, and
sick benefits shall begin from the date of his illness, as shown
by the physician's certificate, and shall furnish such other
documents, attested before a clergyman or magistrate, as may
be required by the Camp, to show the extent and duration of
said illness.

Sec. 48. The funeral benefit, at the death of a brother, shall
be paid to some member of his family, or other person authorized to receive and use the same, and in case there be no such
person, the Chief shall take charge of the funeral.

Sec. 49. If a brother, not three months in arrear for dues,
shall be incapable, by sickness, accident, or injury to his person, of following any vocation, business, or employment
whereby he may obtain a livelihood, as and except as provided
in section 40, he cannot become delinquent. The Chief shall
withhold from such brother's weekly benefits (so long as
weekly benefits shall be payable to him) and pay to the

Financial Secretary, sufficient thereof, to prevent such brother from becoming in arrear for dues and assessments, and thereafter, during such sickness and incapability the Chief shall pay, from the general fund of the Camp, such brother's dues and assessments.

Sec. 50. Every Subordinate Camp shall make provision for carrying into effect, and continuing, the beneficiary character of the Order, by providing for the payment of such weekly and funeral benefits. The weekly and funeral benefits to be paid, shall be fixed by the By-Laws of every such Camp, and shall not be less than fixed and stated therein.

ATTENDANCE ON SICK.

Section 51. The Chief shall appoint a sick committee, who shall arrange to visit each brother reported sick to the Camp, at least once a day during such sickness; *provided* the brother is within a reasonable distance, and not outside the limits of the Camp, and that the disease is not infectious. The Chief shall see that this duty is performed, and that such benefits as the brother is entitled to shall be paid weekly by such committee. If the residence of the sick brother be not less than two, nor more than five miles distant from the Camp meeting-room, he shall be visited at least once a week, by one of the committee, during his sickness.

Sec. 52. Whenever a sick or disabled brother, not suffering from an infectious disease, shall need persons to watch over him, it shall be the duty of the Secretary, when so ordered by the Chief, to notify one or more brethren, as the occasion may require, to watch over him, if within three miles of the meeting-room, and to report at the next regular meeting thereafter, the name of any brother, who shall, for any cause, neglect or refuse to comply with said notice.

Sec. 53. The Chief on receiving information of the death of a brother, shall cause the members of the Camp to be notified to assemble at the proper hour, to attend the funeral and perform the last solemn services.

TERMS, RETURNS, ETC.

Section 54. Terms of Subordinate Camps shall commence

on the first meeting in January in each year, except that the first term of any Camp that shall be instituted after the month of January in any year shall commence on the day of the institution thereof.

SEC. 55. There shall be semi-annual terms ending on the 30th day of June and 31st day of December, respectively, in each year, for which to report the condition of the Camps, and at the end of each such semi-annual term each Camp shall report to the Grand Secretary, in the form that shall be furnished it, the number of initiations, rejections, reinstatements, deaths, contributing members, and the whole amount of receipts and from whatever sources, the names of those suspended and the cause thereof, names of elected officers for the ensuing term, time and place of meeting of the Camp, number of members who received benefits, number of burials of members, and amount paid for same, amount in the treasury, amount invested, and such other information as the Grand Camp shall from time to time require.

SEC. 56. Such returns must be made out and authenticated by the Chief and other proper officer or officers for whose term they shall be made, and by the seal of the Camp, and transmitted to the Grand Secretary within ten days after the end of each such semi-annual term.

SEC. 57. Each Camp shall pay to the Grand Camp a *per capita* tax semi-annually on all active members in good standing.

SEC. 58. If any Camp fail for two successive semi-annual terms to make its returns as required by Section 56, or fail for six months to hold regular meetings, it may be declared defunct and its charter forfeited.

REGALIA.

SECTION 59. The regalia of the Camp shall be selected by the Camp.

The Chief and past Chiefs may be distinguished by three eagle feathers, other officers by two, and members by one, worn in the bonnet.

WITHDRAWAL AND TRANSFER CARDS.

SECTION 60. A brother against whom no charges shall be pending at the time of his application, wishing to withdraw from his Camp, may apply for a withdrawal card, and on payment of all dues, assessments, and fines lawfully charged against or owing by him, including fee for card, he shall at any regular meeting, be granted such card, and shall thereupon cease to be a member of the Order.

SEC. 61. A brother against whom no charges shall be pending at the time of his application, wishing to join another Camp, may apply for a transfer card, and on the payment of all dues, assessments, or dues lawfully charged against or owing by him, including fee for such transfer card, it shall be granted him at any regular meeting.

SEC. 62. A brother holding such transfer card shall pay all dues and assessments to the Camp issuing the card until the deposit of the card by him with some other Camp, which must be done within six months after the issuing of the Card. If at the end of this time he has not deposited his card in some other Camp his name shall be stricken from the books, and his membership in the Camp shall cease, subject, however, to the provisions of Section 64.

SEC. 63. A brother wishing to become a member of another Camp shall make application to it, and present his transfer card within six months. The application shall be referred to a committee of three brethren, whose duty it shall be to inquire. and report at the next stated meeting of the Camp, as to the character and fitness of the applicant, and whether all dues, assessments, and fines charged against or owing by him in the Camp from which he received such transfer card, including Beneficiary dues, have been paid to the day of application to the Camp to which he has so applied. The applicant shall then be balloted for in the same manner as upon the original application. The Camp may also require that the applicant be re-examined by its Examining Physician.

SEC. 64. At the expiration of the time for which a transfer card was granted, the brother holding it, not having deposited it with another Camp, may, at any time within twelve months thereafter, deposit the same with the Camp that issued it, upon furnishing such Camp with an approved medical examination by the Physician of the Camp, duly approved by the

Grand Physician, on the form prescribed for new members, and paying all dues and assessments accruing during the time and up to the date of deposit of the card, and shall be subject to the provisions of Section 63 ; otherwise the brother's connection with the Order shall cease from the date of the expiration of the card, except he be admitted as a new member, in accordance with Sec. 11 of this Constitution.

SEC. 65. The fee for withdrawal and transfer cards shall be regulated by Subordinate Camps, but shall not be less than fifty cents.

TRAVELLING BRETHREN.

SECTION 66. No brother belonging to another Camp shall be permitted to visit a Camp unless he proves himself in possession of the pass-word and shall be examined by a committee, who, on being satisfied, may introduce him.

SEC. 67. No visiting brother can be examined and admitted to the meeting-room of the Camp before the Camp is opened, unless any brother can vouch for the visiting member, and in such case he may be admitted before the Camp is opened.

OFFENCES AND TRIALS.

SECTION 68. *Charges and Committee.*— A member who has reason to believe that another has violated any of the laws of the Order shall present to the Chief a charge against him in writing, specifying the offence, and the Chief, concealing the name of the accuser, shall refer the charge to a committee of three, which he shall appoint. The committee shall forthwith furnish the accused with a copy of the charge, and summon the accused and witnesses to appear before them at such time and place as they may appoint. At the appointed time and place the committee shall meet and hear the evidence, which they shall reduce to writing, and, if called upon so to do, shall produce it before the Camp.

SEC. 69. *Report and Trial.*—The committee shall report, recommending some punishment if they find the charge sustained. The report shall be laid upon the table until the next meeting, at which time the accused shall be summoned to appear, and the Camp shall act upon it. If called for by any member, the evidence offered before the committee shall be read, but no other evidence shall be introduced. The Camp may, however, recommit the case, in order that more evidence may be taken. The accused shall have an opportunity to speak in his defence, and shall then retire. The Camp shall then decide the question, and, if they find him guilty, determine or fix some punishment, after which he shall be notified of the result. The recommendations of the committee may be amended in any manner before final action is taken on them ; and in every case when a member has been found guilty, he shall be punished by expulsion, suspension, fine, or reprimand, according to the character and gravity of the offence.

SEC. 70. *Absence of Accused.*—Should the accused fail to appear before the committee or Camp when summoned, without sending a sufficient excuse, the trial may proceed as if he were present, or he may be punished for contempt.

SEC. 71. *Waiver.*—A member against whom charges have been preferred may, with the consent of the Camp, waive any of the forms of trial, and if he acknowledge to the committee or to the Camp that he has committed the offence, the Camp may forthwith proceed to punish.

SEC. 72. All votes under Sections 68 to 71 inclusive shall be by ballot, and a two-thirds vote shall be required to find a member guilty, or to determine the punishment.

APPEALS.

SECTION 73. Any brother shall have the right to appeal to the Grand Chief or Grand Camp from the proceedings of the Subordinate Camp or the decision of a majority thereof, in all matters connected with the Constitution, laws, and customs of the Order, or on charges sustained.

SEC. 74. When an appeal shall be taken to the Grand Chief or Grand Camp notice of such appeal shall be given at the regular meeting of the Camp at which the decision was made or the trial had, or the next regular meeting thereafter, and the appellant, at the time of giving such notice, shall submit to the Secretary a written statement of the errors complained

of, and the grounds on which the appeal is based, which statement, with the notice of appeal the Secretary shall enter in
the minutes of the Camp. The Secretary shall within one
month thereafter forward to the Grand Secretary a transcript
of the case, duly certified under seal of the Camp, which
transcript shall contain a copy of the proceedings had, the
charges preferred, the report of the committee thereon, the
testimony, the punishment determined or fixed upon, notice
of appeal, and errors complained of. The Grand Chief, or
Grand Camp shall examine and determine the appeal. The
decision of the Grand Chief shall be binding until reversed by
the Grand Camp.

SEAL, MOTTO, LOCATION, MEETING, ETC.

SECTION 75. Every Camp shall have a seal which shall be
used for all official documents. No one shall be authorized to
use the seal except the Secretary, unless by the special direction of the Chief.

SEC. 76. A Subordinate Camp shall not change its location,
as specified in the charter, without the consent of the Grand
Chief. Every Camp shall fix its night of meeting, and shall
not change the same without the consent of the Grand Chief.

SEC. 77. The motto of a Camp may be placed on its By-
Laws, official papers, etc., etc.

SEC. 78. All intoxicating liquors shall be excluded from
meetings of the Camps.

SEC. 79. Subordinate Camps may hold anniversaries or other
celebrations, picnics or parties, and athletic games, and wear
the regalia, without obtaining permission from the Grand
Chief.

SEC. 80. The funds, property, etc., of a Camp cannot be
divided or distributed in any manner among its members
individually, but shall remain the property of the Camp so
long as its charter is unreclaimed and nine Beneficiary mem
bers thereof remain in good standing. A Camp may, however, in its discretion, make an appropriation or donation to
aid a new Camp which may branch from it.

BY-LAWS.

SECTION 81. Each Subordinate Camp shall be fully empowered by a two-thirds vote to adopt such By-Laws as may be deemed expedient, provided they do not in any wise contravene any part of the Laws and Constitutions of the Grand Camp or the principles of the Order,—a copy of which must be transmitted to the Grand Chief, and cannot go into effect until approved by the Grand Chief and the Committee on Laws.

AMENDMENTS.

SECTION 82. This Constitution shall be altered or amended only by the Grand Camp in the manner provided for in Section 64 of the Constitution of the Grand Camp for the alteration or amendment thereof.

DEFUNCT CAMPS.

SECTION 83. In case of the dissolution or suspension of any Camp, any member of such Camp who may be refused or rejected as a member from depositing his transfer card in other Camps shall be preserved as a member at large, receiving no sick benefits, but continuing to pay his assessments, as if regularly connected with a Subordinate Camp, to the Grand Secretary, upon proper notice from said officer, and in case of death his family or dependents shall be entitled to the benefit of the Beneficiary Fund.

Provided, further, that said member shall pay as dues to the Grand Camp three dollars per year in advance, and he shall receive from the Grand Secretary a certificate or receipt authorizing the Chief of any Camp to give him the password in force during the time for which his dues are paid.

Provided, further, that the member or members who are the direct cause of the Camp being suspended shall remain so until after the Camp is reinstated.

The Grand Secretary shall keep a roll of all members at large and their standing in the Order.

TO WHOM PROPERTY SHALL BE DELIVERED.

SECTION 84. Upon being notified of the dissolution of a Sub

ordinate Camp, the Grand Chief shall, in person or through his Deputy, demand the surrender of the Charter, property, and effects of such dissolved Subordinate Camp.

SEC. 85. When a Subordinate Camp is disolved it shall be the duty of its last Chief, or, if there be none, of its last senior officer, or any member or person having such property in his possession to deliver up the charter, books, funds, emblems, uniforms, and other property and effects, to the Grand Chief or his deputy, and any officer or member having the custody of any part of such property and effects refusing to surrender the same, may be forever excluded from membership in this Order, even if his Camp be reinstated.

Suspension of Iniitation During Epidemics.

SECTION 86. Whenever any pestilence or epidemic shall prevail or be threatened in any district where a Camp or Camps of this Order are established, the Grand Chief shall immediately, on in any manner acquiring knowledge of the same, suspend the initiation of new members into said Camp or Camps during the continuance of said pestilence or epidemic or danger thereof. The territory to be prescribed and the period of suspension to be defined by the Grand Chief upon the advice of the Grand Physician.

SEC. 87. All books, blanks, badges, jewels. regalia, uniforms, and emblems used by Grand and Subordinate Camps shall be of the same quality, size, pattern, and material, and in all respects as those prescribed by the Grand Camp.

Section 88.—Order of Business.

1. Opening.
2. Roll-call of officers.
3. Reading and confirming minutes of the last stated and intervening Meetings.
4. Reports of Committees on Candidates.
5. Balloting for Candidates.
6. Initiation.
7. Unfinished Business.
8. Reports of Committees—standing and special.

9.   Communications, Bills, etc., read and disposed of.
10. Proposals for membership.
11. Reports of Sick Committees.
12. Are any Members sick, in distress, or out of Employ-
     ment.
13. New Business.
14. Nomination, Election, and Installation of Officers.
15. Payment of Dues and Assessments.
16. Has the last Beneficiary Assessment been paid.
17. Good of the Order.
18. Receipts of the evening.
19. Closing.

BENEFICIARY FUND AND LAWS OF THE ORDER.

In conformity with Section 65 of the Constitution of the Grand Camp, the Grand Camp ordains the following for the purpose of carrying out the intention of the Beneficiary Fund.

SECTION 89. There shall be a Beneficiary Fund, payable by this Order within sixty days after due proof of the death of an active member. It shall be controlled by the Grand Camp.

SEC. 90. Such Beneficiary Fund shall be divided into two classes, A and B. The brother insuring in class A shall receive at death a sum not to exceed $500 ; in class B, $1,000, payable according to the provisions of Section 89. Provided, however, that if a less sum than $500 is realized on an assessment in class A, such smaller sum shall be the amount paid to the beneficiary or beneficiaries of a member dying in class A. Provided also that if a less sum than $1,000 is realized on an assessment in class B, such smaller sum shall be the amount paid to the beneficiary or beneficiaries of a member dying in class B, as only one assessment shall be levied on account of any death occuring in the Order, but in no case shall the beneficiary or beneficiaries of a member dying in class A, be paid a greater amount than the sum of $500.

SEC. 91. Every applicant for active membership shall be examined by a Physician of the Camp, and shall not be admitted unless on such examination he shall have been found to possess the qualifications prescribed in the Constitution, and evidenced by a certificate of the Examining Physician duly approved by the Grand Physician, in accordance with Section 12 of this Constitution.

SEC. 92. In the event of the death of a brother in good standing in any Subordinate Camp, the amount of Beneficiary, as decided by the Grand Camp at the time of such brother's death, shall be paid as he has directed in his Beneficiary Certificate.

SEC. 93. Any member holding a beneficiary certificate desiring at any time to make a new direction as to its pay· ment may do so by authorizing such change in writing on the back of his certificate in the form prescribed, attested by the Secretary, with the seal of the Camp attached, and by the payment to the Grand Camp of the sum of fifty cents, but no change of direction shall be valid or have any binding foi ce or effect until said change shall have been reported to the Grand Secretary, the old certificate, if practicable, filed with him, and a new beneficiary certificate issued thereon, and the said new certificate shall be numbered the same as the old certificate ; provided, however, should it be impracticable for the Secretary to witness the change desired by the brother, attestation may be made by a Justice of the Peace, or a Notary Public or an officer of a Court of Record, seal to be attached in attest. Every change must be in accordance with the Dominion or Ontario Statutes.

SEC. 94. The assessment shall be collected by the Financial Secretaries of Subordinate Camps, paid over to the Treasurer, and by him forwarded to the Grand Secretary. The names of those who have not paid an assessment, with their proper roll number in Grand Camp, shall be entered by the Financial Secretary on a form furnished by Grand Camp, and transmitted to the Grand Secretary for suspension. The Grand Secretary shall, on receipt of such information, communicate to the Financial Secretary whether the amount agrees with the numbers of the names on his list or not.

SEC. 95. The Secretary of a Camp in which a death occurs shall immediately send to the Grand Secretary a notice according to the form adopted by the Grand Camp setting forth the name, residence, age, date of initiation and death, and the nature of the disease of which the brother died, accompanied by a certificate under the signature of the Chief and seal of the Camp, that the representatives, heirs, or assigns of such deceased member are entitled to the Beneficiary, and stating the amount of all dues, fines, and Beneficiary assessments (if any) remaining unpaid by such deceased brother ; also that the deceased brother was not six months in arrears for dues.

SEC. 96. On receipt of such notice the Grand Secretary shall notify the Secretary of every Subordinate Camp of the

death of such brother, and furnish assessment blanks dated
so far ahead as to give each distant Camp ample time to issue
them to their members, and leave a clear thirty days for collection. The Secretary of each Camp, on receipt of above
blanks, shall call upon every active member of his Camp to
pay, within thirty days, the assessment ordained for the time
being by the Grand Camp ; and, in event of any brother failing to pay, he shall be suspended from his Camp and from all
benefits and participation in the Beneficiary and sick fund,
and shall not be reinstated, until re-examined, at his expense,
by the physician, and certified to be in good health, bodily
and mentally, and on payment of all assessments for which he
may be in arrears.

SEC. 97. Beneficiary assessments shall be levied as fol'ows :
All members belonging to class A shall pay the sum of fifty
cents and those in class B one dollar on every assessment
levied by the Grand Camp whether the death be in class A or
B. When the assessments are collected, the amount to be
paid to the beneficiary or beneficiaries under class A, shall be
fifty cents for every member who has paid in class A and B,
provided always that the amount shall not exceed $500. The
amount to be paid to the beneficiary or beneficiaries under
class B, shall be fifty cents for all members who pay in class
A, and one dollar for all members who pay in class B, provided always that the amount to be paid shall not exceed
$1,000.

SEC. 98. The Grand Treasurer, upon due notice having been
given to him of the death of a brother in good standing, shall
forward the amount of the Beneficiary, as at the time ordained by the Grand Camp, to the Subordinate Camp of which
deceased brother was a member. And the Chief of such Subordinate Camp shall retain from such amount for said Subordinate Camp all unpaid dues, fines, and Beneficiary assessments, if any, owing by such deceased brother at the time of
his death, and all expenses exceeding the final benefit that
may have been incurred by such Camp for the proper interment of such deceased brother, and shall cause the balance to
be paid to the beneficiaries or the legal representatives of such
beneficiaries of such deceased brother, receiving from them
receipts in duplicate properly signed, one of which shall be

retained by the Subordinate Camp, and the other forwarded to the Grand Treasurer.

SEC. 99. Charters of Subordinate Camps failing to pay assessments in forty days may be suspended by the Grand Camp, or, during the interim of sessions, by the Grand Chief, and all members of a Camp so suspended shall become subject to the provisions of Clause 96

SEC. 100. Whenever, after paying a beneficiary, there remains a balance in the treasury, said balance shall be used to pay the Beneficiary of the next death occuring in the order. Should this balance, however, be insufficient to pay a full claim, the Grand Secretary shall call another assessment ; but in no case, shall the beneficiary or beneficiaries of a member dying, be paid a greater sum than an assessment on every member of the Beneficiary Fund in good standing, at the date of the death, would realize, as provided for in Clause 96.

SEC. 101. Brethren wishing to change their Beneficiary certificate from $1,000 to $500 must surrender their original certificate, with the sum of fifty cents to the Secretary of their Camp, who will forward the same to the Grand Secretary, stating the amount to which the brother wishes to change · the Grand Secretary, on receipt of said notice, will issue a beneficiary certificate to the brother in the class named in his communication.

Sec. 103. A member holding a Beneficiary certificate, wishing to insure for a larger amount, must first be examined by the Camp Physician, and have his application endorsed by the Grand Physician, and in all other respects be subject to the requirements of Section 100 before a new certificate will be issued by the Grand Secretary, to whom the member's medical examination papers must also be sent.

RESERVE FUND ARTICLE.

SEC. 103. The fund hereby created shall be known as the Reserve Fund of the Sons of Scotland Benevolent Association, and shall be realized, collected and controlled, maintained, augmented, and distributed or disbursed in the manner and for the uses and purposes hereinafter set forth.

SEC. 104. On and after the 1st day of April next, succeeding the adoption of this article, the sum of ten per cent. in gross of each and every assessment collected from each and every active member of the Association in good standing, shall be transferred from the Beneficiary Fund Account of said Association to the Reserve Fund Account, by drawing an order on the Treasurer of said Association payable to the order of the Board of Trustees, said order to be signed by the Grand Chief and Grand Secretary, with the seal of the Grand Camp affixed.

Sec. 105.   The acting Trustees of the Grand Camp, and their successors in office, shall be and they are hereby declared to be the Trustees of the Reserve Fund.

Sec. 106.   The Treasurer on receipt of said order shall remit by draft to the Grand Chief, who sh ll on receipt of said draft endorse the same and procure the endorsement of the Trustees of said fund forthwith.   The said Grand Chief shall deposit the s me to the credit and in the name of the Reserve Fund of the Sons of Scotland Association in an incorporated Trust company or savings bank, designated by the said Trustees, together with the Grand Chief.   Said Trustees shall meet at the call of the Grand Chief for the purpose of making such designation ; a two-thirds vote being necessary to designate.

Sec. 107.   The Grand Chief and Grand Secretary, immediately on the receipt of an assessment, shall forward to the Secretary of each Subordinate Camp a voucher showing the amount of money contributed to the Reserve Fund under the ten per cent. reduction from said assessment.

Sec. 108.   Whenever the said deposits shall reach or exceed the sum of five thousand dollars, the same shall be invested by the Trustees of the Reserve Fund in Government Registered Bonds, City or County bonds, or in loans on such bond and mortgage as shall be designated by the Board of Trustees, such loans not to exceed fifty per cent. of the estimated value of said real estate.

Sec. 109.   All such securities shall be taken in the name and for the account of the Reserve Fund of the Sons of Scotland, and shall be placed in the hands of the Grand Chief, who shall receipt therefor, and deposit them in an incorporated Safe Deposit company subject to the provisions of such a deed of Trust as shall be approved by the sa'd Safe Deposit company, and accepted by said company from the Grand Chief or Grand Secretary, and Board of Trustees of the Reserve Fund.

SEC. 110. No portion of the said Reserve Fund upon deposit shall be withdrawn for any purpose unless upon a proper voucher signed by the Grand Chief and Grand Secretary, and endo:sed by all the members of the Board of Trustees.

SEC. 111. The Grand Chief and Grand Secretary are hereby required to certify in-writing, with the seal of the Grand Camp attached to all incorporated trust companies or savings banks designated by the custodians of the Reserve Fund, the signatures of the members of the Association who shall have been duly elected and who are duly qualified to perform the duties provided in this article. The Grand Chief and Grand Secretary shall make quarterly reports, giving a complete statement of all moneys received by them on the Reserve Fund account, and shall transmit the same to the Secretaries of each Subordinate Camp in the Order.

SEC. 112. The said fund, as hereinbefore constituted, shall remain intact and undiminished, and shall be increased and added to during the existence of such Association, except whenever in any one year the members shall have paid twelve assessments ; in that case the Trustees of the Reserve Fund shall appropriate so much of said fund as may be necessary to pay the amount due to beneficiaries, in excess of the amount received from such assessments. This payment to be in lieu of an assessment or assessments upon the surviving members ; ex:ept, also, whenever said fund shall have reached the sum of $50,000, and the assessments in any one year to pay death claims have not exceeded said number—then, in that case, the Trustees of the Reserve Fund shall appropriate the surplus of said amount and the interest on the whole of said Reserve Fund, or so much as may be necessary to pay the amount due, to beneficiaries in excess of the amount received from such assessments. This payment also to be in lieu of an assessment or assessments upon the surviving members : always providing, however, that the total minimum amount of this fund shall be five thousand dollars, which amount shall remain intact and undiminished, Moneys over and above this amount only being available for the purposes above recited.

SEC. 113. The Grand Chief and Grand Secretary shall, in addition to their other duties, keep a separate account of said Reserve Fund and a list of all the securities, and shall make a half-yearly report of the same. Said report shall show the amount that has been contributed to said fund during each half year by the ten per cent. transfer—which report shall be published in the half-yearly report of the Association.

SEC. 114. The Finance Committee of the Grand Camp shall, in addition to their other duties, examine the accounts and securities of said Reserve Fund annually, and make a report of such examination to the Grand Camp when in session.

SEC. 115. This Article shall be amended in the same manner as any other Article of the Grand Camp Constitution.

INDEX.

	PAGE.
ADDRESS	2
ADDRESS TO SCOTCHMEN	3 and 4
PREFACE	5 and 6

CONSTITUTION OF THE GRAND CAMP :—

Name and Powers	7
Objects of the Order	8
Time and Place of Assembly	8 and 9
Officers and Elections	10 and 11
Quorum	11
Revenue	11 and 12
Charters	12

Duties of Officers :—

Grand Chief	12 and 13
Grand Secretary	13, 14, 15, 16
Grand Treasurer	16 and 17
Grand Physician	17
Grand Chaplan	18
Other Grand Camp Officers	18
Committees	18, 19, 20
Mileage and Per Diem	20
Order of Business	20 and 21
Returns	21
Beneficiary Fund	21 and 22
Beneficiary Certificates	22
Regalia	22 and 23
Passwords and Circulars	23
Seal	23
Formation of Subordinate Camps	23 and 24
Application for Charter of a Subordinate Camp	24

CONSTITUTION OF SUBORDINATE CAMPS :—

Composition, Powers and Name	25
Meetings and Quorum	26
Membership	27, 28, 29
Officers	29, 30
Duties of Officers	30, 31, 32, 33
Committees	34

Representatives to Grand Camp 34
Fees and Dues 34, 35
Non-payment of Dues 35, 36, 37
Benefits ...· 37, 38
Attendance of Sick 38
Terms, Returns, etc..... .... 38, 39
·Regalia 39
Withdrawal and Transfer Cards· 39, 40, 41
Travelling Brethren 41
Offences and Trials .... ` 41, 42
Appeals.... .... 42, 43
Seal, Motto, Location, Meetings, etc...... 43, 44
By-Laws 44
Amendments... 44
Defunct Camps.... .... 44, 45
To Whom Property Shall be Delivered 45
Suspension of Initiation During Epidemics... 45
Order of Business 46
BENEFICIARY FUND AND LAWS OF THE ORDER... 47 to 54